JIM MASSEY

MASTER YOUR TIME

The Essential Guide to Maximize Productivity, Learn Useful Tips on How To Focus on What Truly Matters and Be More Productive In Your Life

Descrierea CIP a Bibliotecii Naționale a României
JIM MASSEY
    MASTER YOUR TIME. The Essential Guide to Maximize
Productivity, Learn Useful Tips on How To Focus on What Truly
Matters and Be More Productive In Your Life / Jim Massey. –
Bucharest: Editura My Ebook, 2020
    ISBN 978-606-983-584-5

JIM MASSEY

MASTER YOUR TIME

The Essential Guide to Maximize Productivity, Learn Useful Tips on How To Focus on What Truly Matters and Be More Productive In Your Life

My Ebook Publishing House
Bucharest, 2020

TABLE OF CONTENTS

CHAPTER 3

HOW PRODUCTIVE IS YOUR ENVIRONMENT?

CHAPTER 4

DEVELOP YOUR SKILLS

CHAPTER 5

THE PEOPLE AROUND YOU MATTER

CHAPTER 6

PERSONAL TIME MANAGEMENT

CHAPTER 7

MANAGING PEOPLE AROUND YOU

CHAPTER 8

EASY TRICKS TO GREATER TIME MANAGEMENT

INTRODUCTION

If you are reading this book, you are undoubtedly trying to become more productive by managing your time better. That's a great goal. But you can't really manage time. An hour will always consist of 60 minutes, and a day will have 24 hours. That can't be changed. So, if you are lamenting, "I never have enough time!" keep in mind you have the exact amount of time as everyone else.

You can't manage time, but you can manage yourself by making better choices every day. With each choice you make, you can improve your life or make it more difficult.

Proper goal setting is a major part of managing your time. However, it's critical not to confuse your end goal (the final result) with the steps designed to get you there.

For example, let's say your boss has placed you in charge of finding new office space. That's the end goal. But the steps you take to go about achieving that goal will make a huge difference.

You can do research and prepare a list of all available commercial space to present to the boss. This will probably take a few days. And you're not even close to the end goal, which is finding a new office for your particular company. You've started the project, but you've wasted time, as well.

If you were to handle the assignment with an eye on better time management, you would start with a list of needed information. What neighborhood would be best? What is the monthly rent and utility budget? This information can be gathered in minutes (hopefully, from the boss himself) and it will narrow down your project and save you days of needless searching.

Keeping the end goal in mind always saves you time. Have the necessary information at hand *before* you begin the actual work. It will eliminate a lot of steps along the way.

CHAPTER 1

GET TO KNOW YOURSELF

Everyone Has Strengths and Weaknesses

No one is equally good or bad at everything. But if you don't know what your weaknesses and strengths are, you could be blindsiding yourself. Becoming more self-aware is the first step to being more productive.

For example, you may be very analytical, which means you are good at thinking through a problem to the end and seeing solutions. But that same strength could turn you into a perfectionist. If you are a decisive person, you are great at making decisions, but you may not think a problem through entirely before taking action.

When you get to know yourself better, you can amplify your talents and minimize weaknesses. This will help you work at maximum efficiency without wasting time.

They say that we have three selves: how the world sees us, how we see ourselves, and how we really are. To work with and enhance your strengths, make an honest list of what you consider your strengths and weaknesses. Keep an open mind and remain honest. We are all familiar with the favorite interview question, "What are your weaknesses?" The beaming interviewee, of course, answers, "Oh, I always seem to take on too much. I feel like I want to do everything." Can you identify the weakness? Our interviewee is, in effect, stating that she is disorganized and unable to focus on one thing. She cannot manage her time (or, perhaps, her life), properly.

After creating your list of strengths and weaknesses, ask yourself about your general mindset. A mindset is how we view the world. This usually involves pessimism vs. optimism. These attitudes eventually shape our goals and determine how much we get done.

Optimistic people are open to learning and trying new things. That's a critical element to better self-management. You need to believe that being more productive is possible. Optimism, the attitude that things can get done, will help increase your productivity in many ways. Think of it as a secret weapon or a powerful tool in managing your time. It really is true that if you think you can, you will.

That same optimism can help you get the best performance out of those who work for you. Instead of maintaining the mindset of

"This is how we've always done it," you can change people's thinking to, "This is how we could do things better."

To help you gain greater self-awareness, it can be helpful to ask people whom you trust for honest feedback. With so many demands on our precious time, becoming more self-aware is an essential tool for managing your life and your time better.

Determine What You Really Want

It's hard to be productive if you don't know what you want to achieve. What really matters to you? The answer is critical if you want to manage your time better. It's viewing the broad picture that is your life to get the most out of it.

For example, if you determine your family is what matters most, then you will find ways to increase the time you spend with them. If, on the other hand, all you truly want is to be the head of your company, you will know where to devote your time most effectively.

The following exercise can be very helpful. Get a notebook and write down the question:

"If there were no obstacles, what would I be doing right now?"

Ask that questions several times during a week. Don't think or analyze. Just let your pen flow. Or fingers move across the keyboard. This is meant to get the blood flowing and provide you with an insight or two.

Once you've determined what is important, you can start planning your time accordingly. No more wasting the day on small tasks when the important ones are left behind, neglected and forgotten.

What Are Your Daily Habits?

We don't mean to get you nervous, but you may be living with a killer. But not to worry, you can take control of the situation.

Nothing kills productivity and wastes time like bad habits. Bad habits can sabotage your life in the most spectacular way. Habits are the things we do every day routinely, without thinking. It's when we function on autopilot, such as brushing our teeth, driving to work, preparing dinner. Habits are the small things you do every day, and they can add up to the sum of your life.

Let's look at some time-killing bad habits:

1. Not planning each day. If you don't schedule your important tasks, you have no idea what you will be doing on any givenday. Your day will be running you instead of the other way around.

Would you drive across country without a map? You might get somewhere, eventually. But you will likely be taking the long, scenic route. Schedule your day the night before.

Unexpected interruptions do happen, but a schedule will help keep you on track and help you manage your time more effectively.

2. It goes without saying that being disorganized wastes time. Spend a good portion of each hour hunting down the things you need is a major time killer. There is a time management rule that says handle a piece of paper only once. When you check the mail, answer immediately or toss. Don't let paperwork accumulate all over the place like some paper blizzard. Have one specific spot or folder for items to be dealt with at another time.

3. Procrastination steals time from your day the way Billy the Kidd stole money from banks. Brutally and relentlessly. Understand that procrastination is a choice. It's a bad habit, but you have the power to change it.

4. Many of us waste time resisting change. Whether it's preparing a meal in a new way or implementing a new policy at work, change makes us uncomfortable. There is great comfort in the known and predictable. But we will never reach our full productive capability if we don't keep an open mind and remain open to new ideas. Candlemakers were resistant to electricity. That didn't work out well, did it?

5. Are you in the habit of seeing the glass as half-empty? Negativity doesn't only set the tone for the day, but it can truly determine your life. It's been proven that positive salespeople make more sales. A positive mindset helps people perform at a much higher level. Both negativity and positivity begin in the mind. Whether you realize it or not, your thoughts are within your control. The next time you waste time fretting that the boss will hate your report, stop and change your thinking. A positive attitude would be, "I put my best effort into this. It's a good report, even if the boss makes some changes." The less you worry, the less time you waste.

6. When you carry the past into the present, you're toting a heavy load. We all have made mistakes. If you continue to dwell on them, you are slowing yourself down. You can't change the past. You can, however, change your reaction. Simply accept that everyone makes mistakes. There is no need to waste time going over the same memory.

7. Distractions are an obvious time-killer. Modern technology was meant to save us time, however, checking email, social media and other favorite sites can add up to hours of wasted time. The best way to stop being controlled by technology and start to be in control of your time is to have a

schedule. Have a set time to return phone calls. Check email twice a day, and simply turn off any social media functions.

Of course, there are other distractions. Chatting with coworkers, having the boss re-prioritize your work, etc. The best way to handle these is to become aware of who and what it is nipping away at your time. Spend a few days accounting for every interruption. Yes, that will be a bit time-consuming, but the effort will be well worth it. Once you have a clear picture of what or who is draining your time, you can be prepared. If coffee room chats are mounting, bring a thermos from home and avoid the area. If the boss keeps cutting into your to-do list, add extra "spare" time to accommodate his or her interruptions without being thrown off-schedule.

Let's consider your smartphone. Most of us couldn't imagine life without one, and they can be very useful. They can frequently save us time. If misused, however, they can eat up a considerable portion our day. Smartphones can be so addictive, some people seem to have been permanently glued to the virtual space.

Without a doubt, you have encountered the following scene hundreds of times: a busy mother is dragging a toddler through the market while talking on her smartphone. Sure, she is undoubtedly busy, but how is she managing her time. She is trying to do three things at once, namely minding the child, shopping for dinner, and chatting on the phone. You may admire her for "doing it all," but what exactly is she doing? She's not paying the necessary attention to the toddler; she's shopping while being distracted and will very likely forget something; and, she is only able to pay partial attention to her phone call and will miss important parts of it.

Sadly, this busy woman is *not* managing her time well. If possible, she should leave the child with a trusted sitter. If that is not feasible, at the very least she can avoid the distraction of the phone call and pay attention to what she is doing. It's virtually impossible to manage your time well with a cell phone at your ear.

Learning to say no enables you to manage your time more effectively. Productive people are usually eager to do things, but you must know where to draw the line. If you agree to every task someone else demands from you, you will soon become overwhelmed and get less done. Don't be afraid to say, "I'm too busy to handle this right now."

Don't allow yourself to get bogged down with inconsequential details. An estate planning attorney spends at least 15 minutes before each and every will and trust signing contemplating whether to provide a blue or black pen. Others can stew over the best color for labels. Ask yourself, "Does this *really* matter.

Most of us are so used to our own behavior, it's easy to remain unaware of the bad habits that keep us from optimal performance. That's why self-awareness is such a critical time management tool. Awareness is the first step to changing a bad habit into a good, rewarding habit.

CHAPTER 2
DEFINE YOUR GOALS

Many people enjoy being busy. A day filled with random activity gives it a purpose. They become bogged down with trivial minutiae, losing sight of their priorities and totally mismanaging their productivity. Stop and think about why you begin each task before you start. Have a purpose for everything you do. That ensures that every minute of your day will be well-spent. Being busy is not the same as being productive.

Define and prioritize your goals

Start by creating a list. Note down everything you need to do to be effective and productive at your job on a daily basis. That includes anything as mundane as filing away reports.

One of the things this list will tell you is how much time you spend in "crisis management" mode dealing with the problems of others rather than time management mode. While managing a crisis may be necessary at times, this does nothing to advance your own productivity.

On a second piece of paper, create a list of long-term goals. If your goal is to be the head of your department within the next three to four years, what are the steps along the way?

This list may include:

1. Increase profits by 15 percent by end of year.

2. Meet more people in the industry.

3. Meet and interact with more high-level management.

4. Develop a productivity strategy with your boss.

Don't put limitations on your goals. If you're dreaming of running the whole company someday, write it down. You can always adjust, and it's easier to subtract than to add.

Prioritize your list into long-term (president of company) mid-term (meet high level-management) and short-term (finish a report in two days).

Now, determine any and all actions necessary to reach each goal and move up the next step of the ladder. For example, what sub-steps are necessary to increase profits? A different advertising approach? Change in price schedule? A larger staff?

Think about what you enjoy doing and prioritize your likes and dislikes. Go back to Chapter 1 and review your strengths and weaknesses. Are you a numbers whiz? Then that should be your top priority and get the most of your time. Better advertising may be an intricate part of your goal, but perhaps that can be allocated to someone else, freeing up more time for you.

Once you have an idea of how much time you need to spend on each step, make sure it falls in line with your priorities.

If increasing profits is your top priority, one of your steps may be to meet weekly with each salesperson for a review session. But is that a good allocation of your time, or should you institute written reports? Which way will be more productive? Most executives don't have a clear idea of how they spend their time, which means much of it is probably wasted.

Here are some tips for effective goal setting that will help you become more productive:

1. Be sure that your goals are important to you. This may sound obvious, but it needs to be stated. We've already mentioned the need to get to know yourself in order to manage yourself. You may be at a job and have the normal desire to

advance, but if there is no passion, you will never be fully and joyfully productive. If you aren't passionate about your goals, that may indicate you are striving for the wrong goals. That's a wastenot only of time, but of your life.

2. Make sure your goals fit into your life. If you have too many goals, you will have difficulty managing the time for all of them. Time management and goals require a deep commitment. If you cannot totally commit yourself to your goals, you need to start over with your list. Ask yourself, "Why am I devotingtime to this activity? What will be the end result?" Chances are, you won't be heading for the presidency of your company, becoming your local tennis champion, and winning the bake-off at the fair at the same time. As we have stated, time management meant making the right choices for you.

3. Make sure all your goals, and the steps to achieve them, have a firm deadline. It's ok to readjust to accommodate changing circumstances, but a firm plan will help keep you on track timewise.

Make Each Day More Productive

Having goals is a necessary part of managing your time. But you need to take it to the next level and make sure each day is managed to the best of your ability. Don't wait until you're facing a crisis to begin managing your time. Proper time management is a lifestyle and the result of your daily habits. The most productive day is a day *without* a crisis.

Here are some things you can do to get the most out of your twenty- four hours.

1. Develop a productive morning routine. That means getting up early enough for a good, healthy breakfast and some exercise. You are preparing yourself and your body for a productive day, so give yourself needed fuel. This might also be a good time to check your inbox (instead of throughout the day) to see want urgencies await you. Adjust your schedule (you did review your daily schedule the night before, right?) accordingly.

2. If you're unsure of where to start, prioritize your tasks into the most important (top of the list) to the least important (bottom of the list). Getting urgent work out of the way will bring you a huge sense of accomplishment and relief without overwhelming yourself with unnecessary to-do's. We have already discussed how multitasking wastes time and reduces productivity, so complete one task at a time.

3. Schedule your breaks. Breaks are not time wasters. They will give you an added boost to get more done. Taking a five-minute break every 30 to 45 minutes is perfectly reasonable. You gain back the time by being able to focus better.

4. Develop a reward system for having a productive day or a productive week. Studies indicate that 78 percent of people would be more productive if they were rewarded. Be your own rewarder. Plan treats (dinner out, time with friends, a movie) contingent on sticking to your schedule. Something as simple as

26

a gooey dessert can be a great motivator. You need to play fair and *not* indulge in the treat if you didn't produce according to plan.

When Goals Change

Even the best goals can change because ultimately, we can change with time. What seemed like a perfect plan two years ago may no longer be the best use of our time in the present.

The journey of getting to know yourself we discussed in Chapter 1 is ongoing. To maximize your use of time, it should be reviewed each year. Changes are a part of growing as individuals and should be welcomed.

You should start your career with a plan; otherwise, you'll be going nowhere very quickly. However, what happens when the plan no longer suits you? For example, many young law school graduates consider it a dream to start working for a large, prestigious firm. After a few years, reality can hit like a sledge hammer.

Most of them end up working 12 to 16-hour days without ever seeing sunlight for at least 5 years. That's the norm with large companies that work on a 24-hour basis. They are competing with perhaps 25 other people in the same position for that single promotion.

Hard work is always necessary, and managing your time is the best way to get things done. But regardless of how productive you are, maybe the end result starts to look a little less attractive. You work 12-hour days without seeing your family. And you start to wonder if it is worth it. You no longer manage your work; you're simply putting in the time.

This is the point where it may become necessary to reassess and readjust your goals. While you still want your career, perhaps such a mega-environment is not the place to achieve it. Consider different paths to achieving your goal. Going out on your own and opening your own office may still involve a lot of time, but it's time that you'll be able to manage yourself. You get to decide what is important. This path could also provide you with more family time as your spouse spends some time at your side to help you grow.

Don't be afraid to periodically take a good look at where you are going, and, if necessary, take a detour that in the final analysis may have more to offer. You can't manage your time and life well unless you really enjoy the return for your efforts.

CHAPTER 3

HOW PRODUCTIVE IS YOUR ENVIRONMENT?

Eliminate Distractions

Distractions are the modern-day Bonnie and Clyde. They rob of needed time. It's impossible to be productive when you allow yourself to be surrounded by distraction – and, yes, it *is* a choice. While there is little you can do when the boss appears at your office door (we've already discussed scheduling that into your routine), spend a day making a list of the things that eat away your time. Then, eliminate them.

The head of the gang of thieves is, of course, social media. It can creep up on you before you even realize it. Let's say you've rolled up your sleeves and are preparing to work on that major report. Before you begin, you're going to quickly check your emails. That's when you see a notification that your friend has posted on Facebook. No harm in quickly taking a look, is there? On Facebook, you chuckle at your friend's post, then notice a few links to some interesting-looking YouTube postings. Well… since you're here anyway … An hour later, your report is still untouched as you click your way through YouTube.

This happens to everyone. Social media is addictive. People waste hours every day on mindless clicks. You're being robbed, and no guns are involved! Just think of how you could use that extra time in a productive way.

You need to be proactive to keep this from happening. Delete social media apps from your phone. If you need those apps for business purposes, at least disable them when you are working.

It's a natural response to want to respond to texts and messages immediately. Quick responses even rank high in terms of modern etiquette. It's allegedly *rude* not to respond as soon as possible. The fact is, Emily Post never had an iPhone. Let's consider it rude for someone to expect you to stop whatever you're doing immediately and focus your valuable time on them.

Just a single response can ensnare you into a half-hour conversation. Don't fall into the trap. When working, either turn off your phone or engage airplane mode. Return any message when you are at lunch or on break.

Some messages may be work-related and possibly urgent, at least to the sender. Get into the habit of checking your inbox at designated times, perhaps mid-morning and mid-afternoon, but don't let anyone else manage your time.

Distractions don't only happen on social media, they appear in person. Coworkers who are eager for a friendly chat or a distraction in their own routine can appear at your desk unannounced. These can turn into long personal chats from gossiping about a new employee to discussing the weekend's ballgames.

These coworkers are trying to be friendly, but they are interfering with your agenda. Politely, but firmly, tell them, "I'm in the middle of something crucial. How about we talk at lunch?" When managing your time, you need to set unapologetic and firm boundaries and remain in control of your action.

Many of us feel that the more we do, the more we accomplish. We even brag about our ability to multitask.

It's time to take a step back. Our brain isn't geared to concentrate on several things at once. When we try, our attention gets diluted, and we end up concentrating half-heartedly on several things without focusing on one in particular. This is anything but efficient.

Aim for ultimate management of your time by concentrating on one task at a time.

Set a time limit for each task you need to complete, and work within that timeframe. One step, or task, at a time will get you to your goal in the best, more efficient way possible.

You might not have thought of junk food as time robbers, but processed foods and sugars can deplete you of energy very quickly and make you less productive. Ignore the convenient snack machine in the lunchroom and pack some fruit or other healthy snacks for work.

We face distractions everywhere, and few of us make the effort to control them. Once you become master of your own time, you will be less stressed and accomplish more. It's that simple.

Learn How to Focus

Focus is related to avoiding distractions, but it takes it several steps further. It's easy for our mind to wander, even if we aren't being continuously interrupted. We have a lot to do and developing a razor-sharp focus for the important tasks isn't always easy.

Our brain is like any other muscle in our body. If we don't keep it in shape, it becomes sluggish. It can also go in different directions at once. Have you ever tried to focus on a work project while your mind is ruminating about overdue bills, in-law problems, and where to go for dinner this coming weekend? We've all been there. Our mind can turn into a crowded subway train, with no room to act. You feel like you're on a speeding train going nowhere fast.

Focus means control. Control of your thoughts and actions. Proper focusing is a skill that can be learned and developed. Here are some proven methods to hone your focus, manage your time more efficiently, and become more productive.

1. Meditation calms an out-of-control mind. The best and easiest form of meditation is simply to find a comfortable spot, close your eyes, and focus on your breathing as you slowly inhale and exhale. When your mind starts to wander (and it will), return your focus to your breathing. Meditating is one of the best habits to develop when you are trying to achieve self-control. Fifteen minutes to half an hour a day is all it takes, and it is time well- spent. When you are particularly stressed, you can take a "time out" and meditate just about anywhere.

2. While the effect of music on our subconscious is still being studied, there is reason to believe that music does affect our brain, especially the unconscious part. The type of music is probably a personal choice, but it shouldn't be too raucous. Music is abstract, and it is thought that the very abstraction helps the mind stay in focus. It engages us on an emotional level, so our mind isn't racing like an out-of-control horse when we listen. Instead, it is subconsciously processing information and keeping us focused.

Imagine yourself sitting at home when you hear an unexpected noise. Whatever it is, it has your immediate attention as all your focus is immediately directed to the sound you hear. Music works very much like that. It gathers your attention.

You can use music to improve your focus in two ways. The first is to really listen to the exclusion of everything else. The second method is to use earphones and listen to your chosen music while commuting or engaged in some other task. Doing so can help rid your mind of needless clutter.

3. If you are worried about time management, you probably have big goals. And big goals can be intimidating. How do you start that book, that company, or that project? It's easy to become so paralyzed, you don't even start. That's not being productive.

The trick to managing those huge goals is to break each one down into steps, or "chunks." It means understanding what smaller tasks need to be accomplished for you to attain your ultimate end goal. Writing a book may not seem achievable. But writing five pages each day is.

Develop a timeline for each step leading to your goal. Running your own business can seem overwhelming. There's so much to do. Start by identifying smaller, more manageable goals. How will you develop and promote your product or your service? What is your financial plan?

Create a reasonable, chronological timeline for each step that will move you ahead. With each step, you are moving your timeline forward. Have a specific period of time in mind for each step, and work on that step until it is completed. There is a reason for the term, "climbing the ladder of success." It's the steps that complete the journey.

4. Take a break. It may seem contradictory to become more productive by doing less, but our bodies have a finite amount of energy, like a car. We need time to refuel. To get more done in the time you have, take the occasional 15-minute break to regenerate the brain cells.

Have you ever struggled with a problem, just to give up and go to sleep? In the morning, the answer came to you clear as a bell. Some people believe we find answers in dreams. The fact is, the brain can become overloaded. Rest can clear the haze in your mind and allow you to have full clarity.

CHAPTER 4

DEVELOP YOUR SKILLS

There are skills you need for your particular profession, and there are personal skills that will help you manage your time and productivity for any career or task.

The skills you use every day are reading, writing, and speaking. You learned all that in school, and you probably don't even think about how you approach these skills. However, by applying the right techniques, you can make the best use of your time.

Reading

Reading is easy, right? It is, but you need to read a specific way if you are managing your time.

Start with the purpose of your reading. Are you reading for enjoyment, or are you trying to garner information? You probably have different mediums for different needs. You might have one paper for sports, another for editorials, and a magazine for industry/professional information. If that is the case, don't waste time perusing through the rest, unless you are looking for more information.

While reading, skip over certain words that aren't immediately relevant. You want the gist of what is being said. Read the headings to determine whether the information is pertinent. If not, move on to the next article.

Read the beginning and conclusion of any article first. This will tell you whether the midsection is worth reading. Don't waste your time if it isn't.

Remember that the first sentences of paragraphs are usually lead- ins and can safely be skipped for the full information that follows. The opposite will apply if you are unsure if the article has any relevant information that you might need. Skim the first sentences for a quick overview first.

When reading a long article, make a few notes on pertinent important points. This will help organize the information in your mind.

Does this sound like sloppy information-gathering? It isn't. You are trying to determine how much time you should spend on a particular article or book. Once you have a clear idea, you can gather all the information you need and read as much as is necessary. This will save you much wasted reading time as opposed to "properly" reading every word and then picking out the salient points. For better time management, do it the other way around.

Writing

Writing is another skill you learned in school. Unfortunately, few of us are taught to write clearly and concisely. In addition, the use of emails and text have largely eroded what little writing skills are left.

Before writing your report, stop and think about the information you need to convey. Brainstorm and jot down ideas as they come. This will be the beginning of a roadmap that will tell you where you are going and where you need to go to get there. Starting any report without a clear idea will waste time and effort.

After you have jotted down your notes, categorize the information into specific groups. For example, you may wish to categorize a company report into financial information, product information, sales data, departmental responsibility, etc.

Now, you are ready to begin an outline of your report. Before beginning your outline, consider your audience. What information requires the most persuasion? For example, a group of investors will likely be most interested in bottom line financials. A meeting with new employees might need more product information and company structure data.

You are now finally ready to begin writing a clear and concise report. Start with an introduction, move on to the main theme, and wrap it up with a conclusion.

Using headings and lead-in sentences can help clarify the information, as has been indicated in the "Reading" section. It can also help keep you organized.

Try to keep industry jargon at a minimal. Have you ever read a manual, only to wonder whether you are reading Latin? Using clear language and short sentences saves everyone time.

Take the time to edit and review your work, but don't belabor each word. Such perfectionist tendencies will force you to take twice the time necessary to complete your work.

Speaking

Public speaking is a bit more complicated. Like writing, speaking starts with knowing your audience. Who will be there, and what is their purpose? With what information do your listeners hope to walk away?

Once you know your audience, it will be much easier to gear your speech toward their interests.

A speech is different from writing in that you don't get to edit. Your first try is your only chance. But don't be overly concerned about perfection. It's a real time waster.

You should write an outline of the facts you want to hit during your speech. After your introduction, whet your audience's appetite by explaining why your information is relevant to them. How can it help them? Then, tell give them a few verbal "headings" by telling them what you will be talking about, as in, "here is a problem," "here are my thoughts on the problem," and "here's how we can solve the problem."

Prior to actually giving your talk, have several rehearsals, preferably in front of critical family members. You want to be speaking out loud to help you get the tempo and inflections.

No one wants to listen to someone reading a speech, so work from your outline. That's why practicing beforehand is so important.

Reading, writing and public speaking will more than likely become a part of your professional life. When done properly, you can manage your time more efficiently and be more productive.

CHAPTER 5

THE PEOPLE AROUND YOU MATTER

Remember when Mom told you to hang out with the right crowd?

She wasn't just trying to be annoying. She knew some serious facts.

The people around you can make a huge difference in how productive you are. As a matter of fact, the decision of who we spend time with is so important, it should be included in goal setting (feel free to do that).

It's hard not to take on the habits of those around us – whether those habits are good or bad. For the ultimate productive life, choose the ultimate productive people. That will help you manage both your time and your life. Let's take a look at the people who may rob of us of time and productivity. Be aware that this will probably result in you having to make some hard choices. Not everyone currently in your life may be adding to it.

1. Do you know someone who is a complaint marathoner? This person is filled with negativity and will see the glass totally lacking in water every time. According to this person, no one can do anything right. This person can be especially poisonous at the office. Listening to people complain about how bad the boss and job are will drag you down and interfere with your productivity. It will benefit you to drop them by the wayside.

2. Are many of the people in your circle consistently broke?Unless they are still in school or are starting a career plan at the bottom of a long ladder, they are not likely candidates for productivity and good life management. This is not to say you need to drop old friends, but you should probably spend less of your valuable time with them. Seek out people who are already productive and learn their secrets.

3. Some people simply drain you of much-needed energy. They appear to be living in constant drama of Shakespearean proportions. And they expect you to be there to offer a kind shoulder. They will drop by unannounced and call at 3:00 a.m.,

usually drunk. They expect you to spend your time solving their problems.

Anyone can have a crisis. Being there for a friend in need makes you a good person. Being used by a drama queen can trap you into wasting time. Remove yourself from these people for your own sake, even if they are family members.

People Who Can Add to Your Life and Productivity

Productive people should be your role model. Collect as many as you can. Make it a habit to get to know people who manage their time successfully.

Before we discuss how much productive people can add to your success, let's cover an important point. Every office is a place of competition. Employees want to be noticed by the boss, get a raise and the best assignments. And in most workplaces, there is invariably one person who qualifies for all the above. The person who seems to be getting ahead the fastest.

It's easy to resent that coworker. It's even easier to badmouth him or her, try to make him look bad, and assume he is simply lucky.

It's normal to feel resentment and jealousy toward someone who has what you want.

Before you attribute bad qualities to this person, think for a moment. Consider that he or she just might know things about productivity that you don't. If so, this is someone you want as a friend. This does not mean you are using this person. But if you are able to set aside your understandable resentment, you might see that it's hard work and better management skills that is getting this person noticed. This is someone who knows how to manage his or her time and be productive enough to please the boss. This is the type of coworkers that you should be befriending and spending time with more often.

Surround Yourself with Success

When you are with productive people, you will automatically increase your own productivity. There is also a good chance that you'll be more productive while working less. Remember, it's all about better time management.

Productive people have learned how to be organized. If this is something with which you are struggling, what better way to learn than to observe an organized person in action?

Since productive people tend to be more focused, such a person frequently will recognize a problem before it becomes obvious. Fixing a potential problem is a lot less time consuming than trying to repair a huge office disaster. This saves everyone a lot of time.

Find the people in your office who seem to be the most focused, the ones who aren't filling their day with irrelevant tasks. These are the workers that plan ahead and remain in control of their time.

Keep an eye out for people who *look* busy. Frequently, they are the multitaskers. They appear to be busy, but in reality, they waste time and don't get as much done as they should.

Sometimes, people chose to work with such a person because they think they'll look better in comparison. The opposite is true. That person will slow you down to his or her level. You may not always be able to choose with whom you work, but when you do, opt for the productive person. Then watch how he or she works and learn. Productive people tend to make sure those around them are more organized for their own benefit.

CHAPTER 6

PERSONAL TIME MANAGEMENT

Everyone is concerned, and rightfully so, with managing work time. But, we all have a personal life. Personal time is a luxury, and the more organized we become, the richer we are.

Even when we aren't at work, time is precious. We spend around 8 hours sleeping, 2 to 3 hours on chores, and if we have a family, we spend several hours caring for others.

Where do we fit into this 24-hour picture? Is there any time left than belongs to just us?

We need our sleep to remain healthy, so that 8 hours is taken. After spending 8 hours at the office or at work, we are left with another 8 hours, which sounds like a lot. But as we'd seen, most of that time is spent the on chores and obligations. When is there ever time to relax or work on personal goals?

A lot of us may consider time management outside the bounds of personal time. After all, managing our time is work! At the same time, however, we want to get the most out of the time we have for ourselves. That means we need to actively control how we spend those precious hours.

When we are struggling with a career, it is easy to let our personal life take second place. But with the right balance, you can have both. More importantly, you *need* both.

Having a worthwhile personal life takes the same type of commitment as a career. Get your job done and make it a habit to leave the office on time whenever possible. Sometimes, overtime and weekend work are necessary. But most of the time, putting in late and off-hour times is a means to be seen and noticed by the boss. What the boss really cares about is the quality of your work. When you manage your workday effectively, you work less and can leave when you have finished. Forget about strutting around the office at eight o'clock at night in an effort to impress your boss. He or she will be more impressed if the work is done correctly and on time.

Make a schedule of your personal time, the way you would schedule your work routine.

1. Determine your priorities. Do you want to jog, take a class, read a book, watch a movie? Time doesn't simply arbitrarily happen. You need to make the time for those things that are important to you and add to the quality of your life.

2. Once you have a schedule, think about how to free up that time. Do you need a sitter? Will you have to give up some of your favorite TV shows or social media activities? Sometimes, compromise is necessary.

3. Work on your personal schedule before going to sleep, as you would on your business schedule. Make a list of personal things you want to accomplish the following day.

4. Running errands is considered one of the greatest personal time thieves. Make it a habit never to run the same errand twice in the same week. When shopping for food, have a list handy that has everything you need for the week. No more forgotten items that require a second trip. Place all of your dry cleaning in one pile to avoid forgetting an important item.

5. Time is money, and sometimes, it is worth more than money. Consider hiring someone to run some of the errands, such as a neighborhood teen. Having someone come in once a week to do the heavy chores can free up a weekend and be worth the expense.

6. Don't be afraid to ask for help from family. Provide the kids with a list of chores. Have your spouse pick up items from the store. You have more time for yourself when you forget about the idea that you are responsible for everyone else.

7. Spread out needed chores over a few days. Clean the kitchen on Monday and leave the bathroom for Tuesday. That gives you time to relax, catch a movie, or read that book.

8. Planning ahead can give you the gift of time. How often to do run out of batteries, important cards, wrapping paper, stamps,

etc.? These items are difficult to schedule because we don't use them every day. But when we need them, it can absolutely throw us off schedule. Make sure you always have these necessities at hand. Pick them up on your next shopping trip, store them, and simply reach out for them when needed.

9. Make the most of *your* time. Don't just jump in the shower; relax in a hot, scented tub.

Remember – People Matter

Much of our personal time is spent with people we are used to being around. Be painfully honest with yourself and ask who is draining you of energy and time. Does your mother call every evening? Do you have a friend with whom you've gone shopping every weekend for years, but this person adds nothing to your life? Does your neighbor feel free to drop in at any time?

For more fulfilling personal time, we may need to rid our lives of a few toxic people. Gradually remove these people from your life, or limit the time you allocate to them. Making the most of your personal time can mean making difficult choices, but it may be necessary.

Re-Evaluate Your Personal Goals

Much of this book deals with how to manage your time to achieve your career goals. We know that to succeed in a career, we need to establish smaller goals and slowly but surely move up each rung of the career ladder.

How often, however, have you thought in terms of moving up in your personal life? It is easy to take our personal routine for granted. You may run and exercise, read, prepare nutritious meals, etc. But why settle for good when your personal life can get even better?

1. Let's say you run several times a week. Establish an even greater personal goal by training for a marathon. Block out a certain amount of time each time to achieve that goal. Taking the time to elevate personal goals can be life enhancing.

2. If you are already preparing good meals for yourself and your family, go a step further and invest in a gourmet cooking class. The time spent will enhance your enjoyment of food tremendously. Make the time to treat your personal goals seriously.

3. If you read, make your reading material count. Spend your reading time on quality classics that challenge your mind. When we get lost in the desire for a successful career, it's easy to lose sight of becoming a better, more effective person. Take the time to expand your personal goals for a more enjoyable personal life.

CHAPTER 7

MANAGING PEOPLE AROUND YOU

Congratulations. You're the boss. It's an important career step, but the reality is, you are now responsible not only for managing your own time, but that of those people reporting to you. Regardless of how well you do your job, if your team isn't supportive, you are wasting time and manpower.

It's not surprising that studies have found that the most important thing to employees is job satisfaction. They need to know that what they do matters. If they feel unappreciated, they will not work at their full potential, which means they are just wasting time.

Employees who are satisfied with their jobs will remain loyal, which means there will be less turnover and less wasted time spent training replacements. Retaining talented workers is one of best ways to manage your own time.

It is the satisfied employees who will go the extra mile in getting work done on time and solving problems, thus freeing you up to do your own tasks. They are also the least likely to be negative complainers. As we have discussed, negativity sucks needed time out of the workplace.

Office Politics

As the boss, you need to stem politics at the office. This means avoid having "favorites" and creating jealousy among the ranks. Be alert to staff members who continuously feel the need to feed you negative information about others, such as, "The report would have gotten done on time if Mary hadn't been late." The problem here is probably less Mary and more the person who is badmouthing her. When you remain aware of employees trying to undercut each other, you can more easily put an end to the problem.

Not All Employees Are Created Equal

Hopefully, each employee will have his or her own strengths and weaknesses. When handing out assignments, giving the right job to the right person can save a lot time. If you aren't sure of their area of expertise, either make it a point of asking during the job interview or during private meetings. You want your staff to remain motivated. Employees who are able to fully utilize their talents work in a more time-effective way than those who are struggling with the task at hand.

Be Aware of the Workload

People should work hard, but it's counterproductive to overburden them. This is especially true if a selected few (perhaps your better workers) get the lion's share of work while the rest are allowed to work at an easier pace. Assignments should be distributed equally. If someone has problems handling the task, they need to know that they can come to you for help and clarification. This will keep them from procrastinating and doing something poorly at the last minute or making excuses for not doing the job at all.

Create a Positive Environment

Your office is a workplace and should be professional, but a congenial atmosphere helps us to be more productive. It also creates a more open environment for better communication. For example, a Friday pizza-delivery lunch for everyone in the conference room can help people relax. You may find out who is having problems outside the office (a sick spouse or child) and make things easier for him or her by not expecting too much overtime at such a point in time. Such an informal staff get-together also makes it easier for people to mention problems, if only in a joking way.

Create New Challenges

People can easily get bored with the same routine and simply lose interest. That translates into getting less done and more wasted time. Provide new challenges and opportunities for people to grow. An excellent way to open up ideas for new opportunities is to use the informal Friday lunch get-together. Toss out the question, "Anyone have any bright idea of how we can improve things around here?" You might be surprised at the responses.

Compensate Your Employees

Employees who are poorly paid will not work at their full potential, thus wasting the company's time and resources. While there is a need for fair financial compensation, there are other ways to keep employees satisfied. Give credit where it's due and watch that person become twice as productive. If you are unable to manage a bonus, a half-day off once a month is another way to reward your staff for excellent productivity. Think about it. Why would someone work to their full capacity if they have no incentive?

Find Out How Employees Spend Their Time

Even your most diligent workers may be inadvertently wasting time without being aware they are doing so. Have your employees track their time for two weeks and review their schedule. They may be spending too much time on the wrong task.

Don't be Afraid to Delegate

If you need to micromanage everything, you are not being productive. Much of your valuable time will be spent looking over people's shoulders and performing tasks that someone else could and should be doing. That is very bad time management. If you have surrounded yourself with loyal employees, it's smart to use them. Many managers feel that no one can do certain jobs as good as they can. That is limited thinking. If you offer your staff new challenges and train them correctly, it can free up a large chunk of your time that can be put to better use.

Effective time management means knowing when to let go. Start delegating small tasks. As you become more comfortable, increase the responsibility. If you have been following the advice in this chapter, you should be more aware of your staff's strengths. Use that to your advantage and assign new tasks that fall within the range of their capability.

Provide clear directions and let them do the work. Trust them to do the job but do periodically check in and confirm their progress.

Communicate Your Expectations

We've discussed delegating work to your staff, but be sure you communicate your expectations clearly. "I need a financial report on XYZ Company" is far too vague to be effective, and you will likely find yourself disappointed. When assigning a task, be very clear on what you need and when you need it. Confirm that the person is able to handle the task in the timeframe provided. Then, ask to be notified a day ahead of time in the event there are any problems.

This should ensure that you will be provided with the necessary information when you expect it.

CHAPTER 8

EASY TRICKS TO GREATER TIME MANAGEMENT

We hope this book has been helpful to you in managing your time. However, there is still more. There are little tricks you can use every day to get more done in your allotted 24 hours than you've ever imagined.

1. Everyone has the experience of losing papers and spending hours trying to hunt them down. To avoid this, use a folder with a clasp and use a hole puncher for all your notes. Secure them in the folder, where you will always have easy access. Don't leave loose pages laying around. How often has important data mistakenly ended up in the trash?

2. While we're on the subject of notes, if you must go to meetings (most of them are a tremendous time-waster), at least

take diligent notes. That means you won't forget details and can easily ask questions later, if needed.

3. Many people pride themselves on a messy desk as a sign of high productivity. Actually, looking for files and other information wastes a lot of time. Instead, get a small portable file cabinet and place files in there after each use. They will still be at hand, but they won't create needless clutter.

4. If you're in business, the chances are you collect business cards. These cards usually end up in some dark void where you cannot locate them when needed, especially if it's months down the road. Either save business cards in a type of scrapbook, or better, invest in a business card scanner. That way, the information will always be available without you wasting your time looking for it.

5. Consider an alternative to driving to work. Commuting takes time, sometimes an hour each way. A time-saving option would be carpooling or a train. You can discuss business in a carpool, or at least get the daily chat out of the way. Taking a train will allow you to read and make notes and get ahead of your daily schedule.

6. We've advised checking voicemail and email only during scheduled times each day, but we'll make an exception for the following very useful trick. If you are out and discussing business with someone, don't jot names and phone numbers and other vital data on pieces of paper. Call the information into your own voicemail and retrieve the data at a more convenient time. You'll never need to worry about scrambling for names and phone numbers again.

7. When making appointments, always, without fail, read back the time and place of the meeting – "That's Monday, the fifth, at 10:00 a.m. at your offices on 123 Main Street, correct?" You want to be punctual and at the right place at the right time. If necessary, get directions, as in, "Your building is across the street from the shopping mall, right?" No need to waste time in searching for an address.

8. Many people who travel on business absolutely hate doing expense reports. They are a necessary hassle, however. The next time you're on a plane, organize your expenses, receipts, etc. while returning home instead of wasting time on an in-flight movie.

9. Program frequently-called numbers into your speed dial. That saves you time from repeatedly having the punch in the same number. Do it once, and you're done.

10. Improve your time management by asking the boss for feedback. Most bosses are busy themselves and usually don't offer a great deal of feedback. However, it's worth a try, and your boss will appreciate your desire to improve. Ask, "Do you think I could have done the Smith job a better way? Could I have handled in more productively?" The answer will be helpful the next time you're assigned a task, so don't hesitate to ask that question.

11. If you must have meetings, breakfast meetings are the most time-efficient. It ensures you get a good meal and get a head- start on the day. People are usually freshest and at their best in the morning. If you can't go to a restaurant, set up bagels and coffee in the conference room.

12. Avoid scheduling meetings toward the end of the day, when people are tired and itching to get home. You won't have their full attention and may waste time by having to field phone calls the following day to clarify certain points.

13. This may sound like a minor point, but anyone who has ever spilled a cup of coffee over the keyboard or an important report minutes before a meeting knows the panic that can ensue. Work is lost and needs to be redone. If a client is waiting, that could be disastrous. Invest in a spill-proof container and use it, this tip could be a life-saver.

14. A messy computer can waste as much time as a messy desk. Archive old files or save them unto the cloud. You should do a "spring cleaning" of old files at least once a year to remain organized and productive.

Using Time Management Apps

Below are some time management apps that you might find useful. While technology can sometimes be a time robber, these apps are an excellent way to stay on top of your task – a type of electronic nagger.

1. FocusBooster: This app, available for $2.99 per month, helps divide your work into timed session. Set the alarm for half an hour and focus that time entirely on the task at hand. When the alarm sounds, take a five-minute break. You can track your sessions and determine how your time was spent.

2. SaneBox: Your email inbox can be your best friend or your worst enemy. For $7.00 a month, SaneBox sorts your email into folders and separates the important ones from the rest. It also provides a daily summary for your review.

3. 30/30: This is another app, a free one, that lets you divide your tasks into specific periods requiring your full concentration. Then it lets you take a break. Then you can return for another session.

4. Trello is a virtual to-do list that is broken into sections which shift into active, in progress, and finished as you work on

a task. An excellent way for an entire team to keep track of any assignment. The cost is $12.50 annually.

5. Wunderlist is an app that creates to-do lists for your team, with reminders and completion dates. It costs $4.99 per month.

6. Todoist is a to-do list app that allows you to schedule and prioritize your tasks, along with dates of completion.

CONCLUSION

Since there are never enough hours in a day, the better you manage yours, the more time you will have. It takes clear goals and good habits to make the most of your available time. With everything going on around us, wasting time is easy. But with a little bit of effort, you can manage your time like a pro. Review the action steps listed below:

• Know what you really want. It may seem obvious, but frequently, there can be a large gap between what we *actually* want and what we *think* we want. Spend time introspecting about your ultimate goals. It will be time well-spent.

• Create goals. That means lifetime goals, five-year goals, yearly goals, monthly, weekly, and daily goals. Each goal should have the necessary steps to achieve it. The fact is, without clear goals, you will waste a great deal of time. At the same time, remain flexible to making changes when circumstances call for adjustments.

- Review your working environment. Is it geared to saving you time, or wasting it? Make whatever changes you can to optimize your working day.

- We can always improve our professional skills to maximize productivity.

- The people you associate with on a daily basis will have a large impact on how you manage your time. Choose wisely and in your best interest. In some instances, you may need to choose selfishly.

- If you are managing other people, you are managing their time as well as your own. Don't micromanage but understand their work flow.

This book has dealt primarily with managing your business time. However, you have a personal life, as well, and you want to get the most out of it.

You are more productive when you manage your working hours, and the same is true for the rest of your time. You may never have considered "managing" your personal time, but you have much to gain by doing so.

The techniques are much the same. You start with your long- term, mid-term, and short-term goals. These could be a second house, a car, new furniture, or picking up groceries for the evening.

Let's say you want to buy a house. What are the steps necessary that will allow you to do that? First, you need a budget. What items in your life can you eliminate to meet that budget? Are you able to forego weekly dinners out in order to put more money aside?

Then you need to decide what type of house and in what neighborhood. Consider commuting, schools, and other interests. Outlining these steps will help you achieve your goal quicker than you may have thought possible.

The same is true for short-term goals. If you go to the market without a clear idea of what you will be buying, you will be wasting a great deal of time. More than likely, you will also not arrive home with all the needed items, which may mean a return trip. This is wasting a good part of your day.

Start with a list instead. Know what you want and focus on your shopping (that means, no cell phones). By being prepared and focusing on the task at hand, which is picking up things for dinner, you will be done faster and more efficiently.

Managing your personal time allows you to spend more time with family and friends, and that is the ultimate goal of a successful personal life, isn't it? It lets you define your purpose and enjoy the rewards you deserve. If you enjoy hobbies and other forms of entertainment, you will have more time if you plan ahead and actually set a schedule creating the time you need. Many of us go through our personal life hoping haphazardly to fit in some gym time or personal reading time without planning ahead. Invariably, something unavoidable might happen abruptly to ruin our day. With a schedule, you can be better prepared to handle all your personal tasks and still indulge in some luxury time.

Managing your time for greater productivity takes a little effort, but it can bring tremendous rewards. We hope this book will set you on the right path.

Printed by Libri Plureos GmbH in Hamburg, Germany